Hello, Family Members,

Learning to read is one of the most important accomplishments of early childhood. **Hello Reader!** books are designed to help children become skilled readers who like to read. Beginning readers learn to read by remembering frequently used words like "the," "is," and "and"; by using phonics skills to decode new words; and by interpreting picture and text clues. These books provide both the stories children enjoy and the structure they need to read fluently and independently. Here are suggestions for helping your child *before*, *during*, and *after* reading:

Before

- Look at the cover and pictures and have your child predict what the story is about.
- Read the story to your child.
- Encourage your child to chime in with familiar words and phrases.
- Echo read with your child by reading a line first and having your child read it after you do.

During

- Have your child think about a word he or she does not recognize right away. Provide hints such as "Let's see if we know the sounds" and "Have we read other words like this one?"
- Encourage your child to use phonics skills to sound out new words.
- Provide the word for your child when more assistance is needed so that he or she does not struggle and the experience of reading with you is a positive one.
- Encourage your child to have fun by reading with a lot of expression . . . like an actor!

After

- Have your child keep lists of interesting and favorite words.
- Encourage your child to read the books over and over again. Have him or her read to brothers, sisters, grandparents, and even teddy bears. Repeated readings develop confidence in young readers.
- Talk about the stories. Ask and answer questions. Share ideas about the funniest and most interesting characters and events in the stories.

I do hope that you and your child enjoy this book.

—Francie Alexander
    Chief Education Officer,
    Scholastic's Learning Ventures

*For my sister Kathleen Murphy-Gisondi,
who was always inventing
mud pies and more with me!
Special thanks to Jane Gerver for her collaboration
and Cheryll Black for reading over so many drafts.*
—F.M.

*To Ron,
agent and friend*
—D.B.

ISBN 0-439-32238-3

Text copyright © 2002 by Frank Murphy.
Illustrations copyright © 2002 by Dan Brown.
All rights reserved. Published by Scholastic Inc.
SCHOLASTIC, HELLO READER, CARTWHEEL BOOKS, and associated logos are
trademarks and/or registered trademarks of Scholastic Inc.

Library of Congress Cataloging-in-Publication Data

Murphy, Frank, 1952-
    Always inventing : the true story of Thomas Alva Edison / by Frank Murphy ;
illustrated by Dan Brown.
        p. cm.— (Hello reader! Level 3)
    ISBN: 0-439-32238-3 (pbk.)
    1. Edison, Thomas A. (Thomas Alva), 1847-1931—Juvenile literature. 2.
Electric engineers—United States—Biography—Juvenile literature. 3. Inventors—
United States—Biography—Juvenile literature. [1. Edison, Thomas A. (Thomas Alva),
1847-1931. 2. Inventors.] I. Brown, Dan, 1949- ill. II. Title. III. Series.
TK140.E3 M84 2002
621.3'092—dc21
[B]   2001031347

20 19 18 17 16 15 14 13 12   08 09 10 11 12

Printed in the U.S.A.
First printing, April 2002

23

Always Inventing
The True Story of
THOMAS ALVA EDISON

by Frank Murphy
Illustrated by Dan Brown

Hello Reader! — Level 3

SCHOLASTIC INC.

New York   Toronto   London   Auckland   Sydney
Mexico City   New Delhi   Hong Kong   Buenos Aires

The year was 1847.
The winter was cold and snowy.
The place was a little town in Ohio.
Inside a snow-covered, redbrick house,
a baby boy was born.
His parents named him Thomas Alva Edison.

Most babies cry a lot,
but Thomas hardly ever cried.
Instead, he cooed and laughed a lot.
Baby Thomas was different in another way, too.
He looked like he had questions to ask.
But baby Thomas couldn't talk yet.

Just a few years later, though,
Thomas was busy asking questions.
When someone didn't know an answer,
Thomas tried to discover
the answer himself.

One day when Thomas was three years old,
he was helping his mother in the barn.
They were gathering eggs.
He noticed a goose sitting on some eggs.
He wondered how the goose
would make the eggs hatch.

Thomas wanted to see if he could
hatch some eggs himself.
He made a nest with straw and hay.
He filled it with eggs.
The chickens and geese stared at Thomas.
Thomas bent down.
Then he sat down on the eggs.

CRACK! SPLAT!
Thomas looked down at the eggs.
Thomas looked at his bottom.

EWWW!
What a mess!

Thomas's questions always
led to experiments.
When he was just six years old,
one of his experiments got him into trouble.
Thomas wanted to see how fire burned.
He was in his father's barn.
Thomas didn't mean to, but he burned
the barn down.
His father was mad!

Still, Thomas wanted to do experiments,
so his mother let him do them.
She even bought him a science book.
But since Thomas was messy,
he had to do his experiments in the basement.
Many times his mother heard strange sounds.
She sniffed strange smells.
Thomas was busy answering his questions!
But was the house safe?

Thomas didn't want to burn
the house down.
And he didn't want to
get in trouble anymore!
Plus he needed money for
more chemicals and materials
to do his experiments.

So when Thomas was 12 years old,
he got a job at a railroad station.
He worked on a train.

Thomas sold things to the passengers.
He sold candy.
He sold fruit.
He sold newspapers.

But he couldn't stop experimenting.
In the corner of a boxcar, he built
four shelves and a small table.
He filled the shelves with bottles
of chemicals.
He laid tools on his table.
This was Thomas's new laboratory.

One day, when Thomas was
using some chemicals,
the boxcar rattled and shook.
One of the bottles fell to the floor.
BOOM! An explosion!
Thomas had started another fire!
He tried to stomp the fire out
with his shoes.
Then a baggage man helped Thomas
put out the fire.
The baggage man
also threw out the chemicals.
Luckily, no one was hurt.
That was the end of Thomas's experiments
on a train.

One day someone almost got
hurt very badly.
But it wasn't from one of
Thomas's experiments.

It was 1862, and Thomas was 15.
Thomas saw a small boy
named Jimmy playing near
the railroad track.
Thomas looked the other way
and saw a train rolling
toward Jimmy.

Thomas threw down his things.
He ran and grabbed little Jimmy.
Then Thomas pulled Jimmy away
just as the boxcar whisked by.

Everyone at the railroad thought Thomas was a hero—especially Jimmy's father.

To reward Thomas for his good deed, Jimmy's father gave Thomas a better job working with a telegraph machine. It was a machine that sent and received bits of sound that stood for letters. A telegrapher figured out what the bits of sounds meant. People all over the country communicated with telegraphs.

Now Thomas had a job that
paid more money.
That meant more experiments!
Thomas also learned more about wires
and machines and electricity.

In 1876, a man named Alexander Graham
Bell invented the telephone.
When people spoke into the first telephones,
their voices sounded scratchy and unclear
to the person on the other end.
Messages were difficult to understand.

Thomas wanted to make the telephone sound better so people could talk to each other all of the time.

One year later, Thomas invented a transmitter. It had little pieces of carbon inside that made voices sound louder and clearer. The telephone became more helpful and easier to use.

Thomas knew he could invent even greater things!

In the 1870s, people used candles and
lanterns to light their homes.
Sometimes the candles and lanterns
tipped over and started fires by accident.
This was dangerous.

Thomas always remembered the sad story
of The Great Chicago Fire of 1871.

In a barn, a cow had kicked over
a lighted lantern.
A fire started in that barn.
The fire spread across the city.
It burned for a whole day.
Almost the whole city was burned.
More than 17,000 buildings burned
to the ground.
More than 300 people died.

Thomas remembered his own mistakes
with fire years before.
He knew that fire was dangerous.
He thought, "How can we light homes
in a safer way?"

Thomas remembered, as a child, reading
about Ben Franklin.
Ben had experimented with electricity
in the 1700s.
He had proved that lightning was electricity.
Thomas wondered, "If electricity could
make lightning so bright, then could it be
used to light homes?"
He had to find out how!

Thomas read and read.
He wrote and wrote.
He experimented and experimented.
Thomas connected wires that went
into a glass ball.
At the end of the wires, he twisted
tiny threads of cotton into a thin,
but strong, wire.
He sent electricity through
the wires and thread.

The thread burned brightly.
Finally, Thomas had done it!
He had invented a small glass ball
that glowed with light—a lightbulb!

People were excited about Thomas's invention.
But his work wasn't done.
He had to help people get electricity into
their homes so they could use the lightbulbs.
It took many more years of experiments and
inventions—light switches, tools that
measured electricity, and wiring, too.

Finally in 1882, Thomas invented a network
of devices—switches, generators, sockets,
and wires.
The devices sent electricity to homes
in a neighborhood of New York City.
The lights went on in 85 homes!

Soon, giant electric generators—
called "power plants"—
were built all over the world.
Thomas's inventions helped
to light up the whole world!
Thomas was a hero again!

Thomas invented other important things, too.

A movie camera.

A movie projector.

A copy machine.

A phonograph.

A talking doll . . .
and more!

Thomas was always inventing!
He built more than 1,000 inventions!
Many of his inventions led to better
inventions that we use today.
He made our world a safer place.
He made our world a brighter place.
He made our world a better place!

Thomas died in 1931.
He was 84 years old.
People were sad.

But they celebrated Thomas Edison's life. At ten o'clock on the night of his funeral, people remembered him.
Everyone across the United States turned off their lights—and said good-bye to Thomas Alva Edison at the same time.